TOO OLD FOR MYSPACE
TOO YOUNG FOR MEDICARE

Other Books by Joey Green and Alan Corcoran

Hellbent on Insanity
You Know You've Reached Middle Age If . . .
Senior Moments
Champagne and Caviar Again?

Other Books by Joey Green

The Gilligan's Island Handbook
The Get Smart Handbook
The Partridge Family Album
Polish Your Furniture with Panty Hose
Hi Bob!
Selling Out
Paint Your House with Powdered Milk
Wash Your Hair with Whipped Cream
The Bubble Wrap Book
Joey Green's Encyclopedia of Offbeat Uses for Brand-Name Products
The Zen of Oz
The Warning Label Book
Monica Speaks
The Official Slinky Book
The Mad Scientist Handbook
Clean Your Clothes with Cheez Whiz
The Road to Success Is Paved with Failure
Clean It! Fix It! Eat It!
Joey Green's Magic Brands
The Mad Scientist Handbook 2
Jesus and Moses: The Parallel Sayings
Joey Green's Amazing Kitchen Cures
Jesus and Muhammad: The Parallel Sayings
Joey Green's Gardening Magic
How They Met
Joey Green's Incredible Country Store
Potato Radio, Dizzy Dice
Joey Green's Supermarket Spa
Weird Christmas
Contrary to Popular Belief
Marx & Lennon: The Parallel Sayings
Joey Green's Rainy Day Magic
The Jolly President
Joey Green's Mealtime Magic
The Bathroom Professor: Philosophy on the Go
Famous Failures
Joey Green's Fix-it Magic

TOO OLD FOR MYSPACE

TOO YOUNG FOR MEDICARE

Joey Green and **Alan Corcoran**

Andrews McMeel
Publishing, LLC

Kansas City

For Debbie and Theresa, who have yet
to reach middle age and never will.

09 10 11 12 TEN 10 9 8 7 6 5 4 3 2

ISBN-13: 978-0-7407-7108-8
ISBN-10: 0-7407-7108-6

Library of Congress Control Number: 2007933999

www.andrewsmcmeel.com

Attention: Schools and Businesses
Andrews McMeel books are available at quantity discounts with
bulk purchase for educational, business, or sales promotional use. For information,
please write to: Special Sales Department, Andrews McMeel Publishing,
1130 Walnut Street, Kansas City, MO 64106.

Introduction

Well, it finally happened. You can't put your finger on exactly when, but you're definitely no longer a spring chicken. Did it become apparent the day you traded your Harley for a Winnebago? Or the afternoon you spent fruitlessly looking for Dockers that didn't make you look like your dad? Maybe it infected you like a computer virus unsuspectingly attached to that first e-mail from the AARP.

No matter. At least it's not "creeping up on you" anymore.

It's officially here. Thinning out your hair, blurring your vision, turning your buns of steel into blubber. It's like you hit 100,000 miles and now your transmission is falling apart. Wave good-bye to your youth, your libido, and your hairline as they recede in the rearview mirror of your minivan.

Welcome to Middle Age.

Travel with us, dear reader, as we traverse the terrain of the flabby-armed, baggy-eyed, and shaggy-backed. The time when a young man's fancy turns into an old man's creepiness. It's the last rest stop on the road of life, and there's a long line at the bathroom. You're too old to rock and roll and too young to die . . . actually, you've come to the awful realization that death doesn't discriminate by age. Let's just say you're too old for Facebook, too young for a face-lift. Too old for low-rider jeans, too young for a low-salt diet. Too old for hip-hop, too young for a hip replacement.

It's not pretty, but at least you've got lots of company. Every two seconds another baby boomer hits middle age. In fact, today 200,000 baby boomers will celebrate a birthday (not bad if you own stock in a birthday candle company). This year alone, four million baby boomers will turn fifty. That's a lot of people going over the hill at the same time, all looking to buy beachfront property, reserve an eight o'clock tee time, and find an inexpensive way to refill their prescription for Viagra. True, you're not alone, but you're definitely aboard the Old Fart Express Bus.

If you think you've somehow managed to escape the horrors of middle age, we've compiled this handy catalog of the telltale signs. So belly up to the Barcalounger, loosen your Levi's (nice look, Pops), and join us on our geriatric journey. Sit up straight (if you're back doesn't hurt too much), put on your reading glasses (if you can find them sitting on top of your head), and make sure you've got plenty of light.

And don't worry too much about being middle-aged. Eventually you'll grow out of it.

TOO
OLD FOR
MYSPACE
TOO YOUNG
FOR
MEDICARE

You received three
birthday cards, and one
was from your dentist.

• • • •

Even though you write down
all your appointments on
a large desk calendar, you
completely forget about them.

You take more vitamins
than there are letters
in the alphabet.

Your shoes have
Velcro tabs
instead of laces.

•   •   •   •

You've used the phrase
"I don't need a lecture."

You remember the name of George McGovern's running mate.
Both of them.

• • • •

You think Hannah Montana is the name of a city.

You have your entire collection of Beatles, Rolling Stones, and Bob Dylan albums in a cardboard box in your attic.

• • • •

You can't figure out the Department of Agriculture's new food pyramid chart.

• • • •

You own a bridge table and four folding chairs.

You tried to save money by installing the new tile in the bathroom yourself, but you ended up spending $1,000 on visits to the chiropractor.

You've got a box in
the garage with thirty-one
AC adapters that you are
never going to throw away.

You know who
Eddie Haskell is.

You haven't changed
the recorded message on
your answering machine
since 1996.

• • • •

You know what
"analog" means.

You let your annual membership to the gym renew itself automatically on your credit card even though you haven't been there since you first joined.

You have a box full of 8mm videotapes of your home movies that you've been meaning to convert to DVD.

You haven't seen your closest friends since your twenty-fifth high school reunion.

• • • •

You've had a meaningful conversation about life with a carpet salesman.

**At Christmastime,
you leave a greeting card
and a twenty-dollar bill in
your mailbox addressed
to your mailman.**

• • • •

**You rate your day by
the number of trips you've
made to the bathroom.**

You bought a book you think you've read before. After rereading the whole thing, you're still not sure.

• • • •

Been everywhere, done everything.

You know that the correct screwdriver is the largest one that fits—especially for a Phillips head.

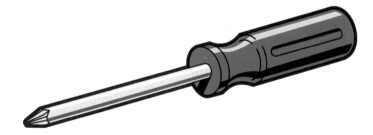

Your next real estate investment will be about three feet wide and six feet deep.

You're living in a house with five bedrooms, four televisions, three bathrooms, and two people.

You've bought *Dark Side of the Moon* on vinyl, eight-track, cassette, CD, DVD, and MP3.

• • • •

Your garage is a museum of obsolete electronics of the past forty years.

You know how to tie-dye.

• • • •

You already know
what the "first thing to go"
is . . . and the second
and the third.

You're no longer in a demographic group coveted by advertisers, with the possible exception of Polident and Forest Lawn.

• • • •

You have a remote control that controls your remotes.

The Environmental
Protection Agency has
declared your ear hair a
protected ecosystem.

• • • •

A May-December romance
is pretty much your only
option at this point.

Your life insurance company
uses six supercomputers to
calculate your premium.

You've hesitantly eaten
a Thanksgiving turkey
cooked in a microwave oven.

You've risked the dangers of Clackers and witnessed the Footsee phenomenon.

• • • •

You've suffered the embarrassment and shame of putting in the carbon paper backward.

You know that most pants max out at a forty-eight-inch waist, but some go up to fifty-two inches.

• • • •

Your beer is whatever Costco is selling for $4.95 a case.

When asked for an
Allen wrench, you reply,
"inches or metric?"

• • • •

You've been practicing
"Welcome to Wal-Mart"
as your backup
retirement plan.

The history of dental technology can be traced from your bicuspids to your incisors.

• • • •

You're secretly proud that you outscored your kid on the SATs.

• • • •

You have no plans to buy another car, even though your odometer is into six figures.

You're surprised that people older than you actually want to run for president.

• • • •

Your 401(k) has just about 401 Ks in it.

• • • •

You are down to three vegetables you can fully digest.

Your fantasies now involve retirement instead of starlets.

• • • •

Sex, drugs, and rock 'n' roll? Well, you'll always have drugs. By prescription, anyway.

You refuse to confront
your mortality until Keith Richards
dies—or at least stops touring.

• • • •

You're pretty sure that if there
really was a Greatest Generation,
it wasn't yours.

• • • •

Too young for mah-jongg,
too old for Mario Brothers.

**Your financial planner
recommends you retire
two years after you're dead.**

• • • •

As far as you're concerned,
a GPS unit takes all the
adventure out of driving.

• • • •

**You know it's just a matter of time
before you hear a song
by Rage Against the Machine
in the elevator.**

You think it's funny that
Paul McCartney still plays
"Helter Skelter" to prove
he's a badass.

• • • •

You've noticed that
the same pricks who were
the hall monitors in
grade school are now
running the country.

You've had to explain that your drooling resulted from a **BOTOX** mix-up and will improve after six months.

You've decided that no college degree is worth $160,000, but it's too late now to back out on your son.

You've got four shelves of camping gear that haven't made it out of the garage since the Carter administration.

● ● ● ●

The waitress always brings you the check.

● ● ● ●

Now that you can print stamps from your computer, you don't have anything to mail.

The *Los Angeles Times* has determined that you are its last subscriber.

● ● ● ●

You remember when the only special effect needed to make a blockbuster movie was a twenty-five-foot mechanical shark.

You figure the five-digit
zip code is good enough.

•   •   •   •

You've divided technology
into two categories:
"better if it's bigger"
and "better if it's smaller."

You threw out all of your computer diskettes once you realized you didn't have anything that could read them anymore.

It takes you an hour
to compose and send
a text message on
your cell phone.

• • • •

Too old for birth control,
too young for
bladder control.

You remember when you didn't need a Social Security number until you got a job.

You wonder why Janis and Jimi are gone but Frampton is still alive.

You've calculated that you
could retire right now
if you could learn to live
like Ted Kaczynski.

You can't prove it, but
you're pretty sure
the world has gotten
a lot more uptight.

First you didn't trust anyone over thirty, now you don't trust anyone under thirty.

• • • •

You know that the fish cheer did not always celebrate our finned friends.

You remember when there were nine planets, forty-eight states, and one evil empire.

You're nostalgic for the good old days when all we had to worry about was nuclear annihilation.

You remember when no one had health insurance and nobody cared.

You're not sure which is the greater technological achievement: the moon landing or ATMs.

• • • •

You remember when the Fastpass at Disney World was called the E-ticket.

You recall a time when
you didn't have to be
an Idiot or a Dummy
to buy a book.

• • • •

You went through childhood
without an infant seat,
air bag, or seat belt—
and lived to tell about it.

You remember having to go
to a neighborhood theater
to see porn.

•　•　•　•

You know which cigarettes
were a "silly millimeter longer,"
which ones you'd "walk a mile"
for, and for which ones you'd
rather "fight than switch."

You remember when AT&T was a gigantic telephone monopoly—the first time around.

●　●　●　●

You're pretty sure there was no Composite Materials merit badge when you were a Boy Scout.

●　●　●　●

You didn't know what a latte was until you were thirty-five.

You can't decide whether to replace your personal trainer or your hip.

Your refrigerator has crushed ice, a soft-drink dispenser, and an Internet connection, but it still can't remind you why you opened it in the first place.

If Woody Allen can marry Soon-Yi, you figure you still have a shot at Lindsay Lohan.

• • • •

Your iPod contains mostly *Harvard Business Review* audio books and MPEGs of 1970s Grateful Dead concerts.

**Errant seeds and
stems still emerge
from the seams of your
Bob Marley albums.**

• • • •

**Online dating seems
like call girls
with lower prices.**

You're still holding out hope for a Supertramp reunion.

• • • •

You no longer hate the Man because now you *are* the Man.

You're convinced that
iTunes lacks the timeless
sweet karma of the mix tape.

You've started to
express a thought and in
midsentence forgot what
you were going to say.

You remember when
a cup of coffee cost a
quarter and came in only
one size and one flavor.

• • • •

You remember
when classrooms had
chalkboards.

You know what a filmstrip is.

• • • •

You remember when
cameras had film.

• • • •

You receive credit card
offers in the mail at least
once a week.

You remember when spam referred to canned luncheon meat.

• • • •

You know who Brian Jones was and how he died.

You're on a first-name basis with your child's school principal.

• • • •

You remember when a flight attendant was called a stewardess, a firefighter was called a fireman, and a postal carrier was called a mailman.

You've had your cat both fixed
and put to sleep.

You know how to prune
a rosebush.

The AARP has described you
as a "person of interest."

You've given up on living vicariously through your children. Now it's up to your grandchildren.

• • • •

You've traded in the minivan for a golf cart.

• • • •

You've got a 28 handicap and an $8,000 set of clubs.

There's cough syrup
in your medicine cabinet
that expired during the
swine flu scare.

Over the past ten years
you paid $130,000
to reduce your mortgage
principal by $3.12.

• • • •

You once filled your
tank for five bucks and
got a free drinking glass
from Mobil.

You wish you had saved
your seventies clothes to aid
in your insanity defense.

Your lawyer, doctor,
and accountant have
all retired and referred
you to their sons.

You can't grow a decent tomato, but 142 new species of dandelions have been discovered on your front lawn.

Your daughter borrowed more money to go to law school than you paid for your first house.

• • • •

You'd rather pay your kids' rent than have them move back home.

Old kitchen utensils never die, they just get redeployed to the RV.

• • • •

Nobody lives forever, but you're still convinced you stand a good chance.

One pill makes it hard and one pill makes it small, but the ones advertising on television make you want to do it in twin bathtubs on the beach.

• • • •

You knew Al Gore wasn't going to win when you found out he had married a girl named Tipper.

You remember when Welch's Grape Jelly came inside free Flintstone drinking glasses.

• • • •

You know what paraquat is.

• • • •

You remember when a pocket calculator cost more than a television set.

You own a
Bay City Rollers album.

●　●　●　●

You remember being scared when
Skylab fell back to Earth.

●　●　●　●

You made beaded curtains
made from flip-top lids.

You owned a Pet Rock.

• • • •

You once took a date
to a movie in Sensurround.

• • • •

**You owned a pair
of Earth Shoes.**

You've experienced
the incredible high of
recarpeting your home.

• • • •

You remember a time when
you had to go to the bank
on Friday if you wanted
cash for the weekend.

You remember the birth
of the smiley-face button.

It's Never Too Late

At 60

Frieda Birnbaum gave birth to twins.

At 62

J.R.R. Tolkien published the first volume
of *Lord of the Rings*.

At 63

Satirist Jonathan Swift wrote
"A Modest Proposal."

At 66

Feminist Gloria Steinem
got married for the first time.

At 70

Benjamin Franklin helped draft the
Declaration of Independence.

At 75

Cancer survivor Barbara Hillary became the first black woman to reach the North Pole—on skis.

At 80

Jessica Tandy became the oldest person to receive an Academy Award—for her role in *Driving Miss Daisy*.

At 81

William Painter became the oldest climber to reach the 14,411-foot summit of Mount Rainier.

At 82

Johann Wolfgang von Goethe
finished writing *Faust*.

At 83

Shimon Peres was elected president
of the State of Israel.

At 87

Mary Baker Eddy founded the
Christian Science Monitor.

At **89**

Claude Pepper became the oldest person ever elected to the U.S. House of Representatives and chaired the U.S. Bipartisan Commission on Comprehensive Health Care.

At **90**

U.S. Senator Robert C. Byrd was the longest-serving senator in the nation's history.

At **93**

Strom Thurmond was re-elected to the U.S. Senate.

You know what
cyclamates are.

● ● ● ●

You've used
the catchphrase
"Flick my Bic."

For entertainment,
you read books.

• • • •

You have an IRA,
a Roth IRA, and
a SEP-IRA.

Your greatest battle in life is trying to kill all the algae in the pool.

You once owned a video camera the size of a bread box.

You remember when a man in a uniform filled your car with gas, checked your oil, and cleaned your windshield—all for under five dollars.

You can't tell the difference between an LCD and a plasma-screen TV.

Now that you can afford to buy any electric guitar your heart desires, you have no interest whatsoever.

You were tempted to parachute from an airplane—until you realized that your life insurance policy won't pay if you go splat.

• • • •

Every time you go to Costco, you forget to bring your membership card.

You still refer to Russia
as the Soviet Union.

• • • •

You plan your spontaneous
road trips two months
in advance by going to the
AAA office and having them
map the trip for you.

You can't remember
anyone's name anymore.

● ● ● ●

You know the
difference between
Lipitor and Crestor.

You have no desire to see any of the *Harry Potter*, *Pirates of the Caribbean*, or *Spider-Man* movies, but you'd gladly sit through a *Planet of the Apes*, *Godfather*, or *Back to the Future* marathon.

You've played "Big Bucks Bingo"
on a Royal Caribbean cruise ship.

• • • •

You've owned more than
seven vacuum cleaners.

• • • •

You own a carbon monoxide alarm.

You change the oil on your car every 4,000 miles, but you can't remember to rotate your mattress once a year.

•   •   •   •

You've lost your voice from screaming from the sidelines of a kids' soccer game.

•   •   •   •

You shop around for the best place to fill your prescriptions.

You know the difference between white, wheat, multigrain, and seven-grain bread.

You were delighted to see Paris Hilton go to jail and cry for her mommy.

You can actually taste
the difference between
chardonnay, cabernet
sauvignon, and pinot noir.

You've hidden the key
to your liquor cabinet
and had to call a
locksmith to open it.

Your passport photo looks
like the child of your
driver's license photo.

You remember when Coca-Cola was available in only one flavor.

• • • •

You've used the expression "Because I said so."

You've lusted after the soccer mom with the boob job, bleach-blonde hair, low-rider jeans, and tube top.

You've filled it to
the rim with Brim.

•　•　•　•

You remember when
granola was some kind of
hippy-dippy health food.

You have ten pairs of
reading glasses hidden
around the house.

• • • •

You buy postage stamps
one hundred at a time.

You own a Rubbermaid
container filled with
beach toys.

When twentysomethings
talk about hooking up, you
think they're getting cable.

You've been screwed over by the "lifetime guarantee" several times.

• • • •

When you play Monopoly, you insist upon playing strictly by the rules.

You own the deluxe
turntable version of
Scrabble.

The bank where you opened
your first checking account
went out of business.

You know what
KFC stands for and you
remember when the
Colonel was alive.

• • • •

You know who
Frankie Valli and the
Four Seasons were.

**You watched Tiny Tim
marry Miss Vicki.**

• • • •

**You've sat through a high
school graduation ceremony
of one of your offspring.**

• • • •

**You've gone to an
art museum for fun.**

You remember when a video game
consisted of two paddles
and a square ball.

• • • •

**You can make yourself look
ten years younger with a shave
and a haircut.**

• • • •

When you compare reality to
reality TV, reality always wins.

You've compared the relative comfort of husky trousers from Haggar, Dockers, and Levi's.

● ● ● ●

You watched the original broadcast of the final episode of *M*A*S*H*.

You don't buy anything
on credit.

You still wear a wristwatch,
even though you can check
the time on your phone.

First you became your
own personal trainer, now
you've become your
own personal doctor.

. . . .

You remember
when headphones
didn't need batteries.

If you'd had any idea there was so much money to be made in hedges, you'd have majored in botany and horticulture.

You watch your weight,
but it goes up anyway.

Your contribution to
greening the planet was
replacing your Malibu lights
with the solar-powered kind.

You took a picture of your
ear hair when you tried
to answer your
multifunction cell phone.

● ● ● ●

You've priced security cameras.

● ● ● ●

If it involves special
footwear or protective gear,
you're not playing.

You've narrowed down your
choice of breakfast cereals
to a single brand that
you have been eating
for the past ten years.

You've noticed that poker
is less fun when you
eliminate the smoking
and drinking part.

You've realized that the eight-story-high IMAX screen is almost as big as the screen they used to have at the movie theater when you were a kid.

You liked *Extreme Makeover* the first time around, when it was called *Queen for a Day*.

• • • •

The decline in your eyesight is conveniently offset by the ascent of high-definition television.

You wonder why all other countries have bullet trains, and all we have are bullets.

Between outwitting the competition, avoiding the tax bite, protecting your nest egg, and battling City Hall, who needs video games?

You're convinced microwave ovens were created because their feasibility as weapons didn't pan out.

•   •   •   •

You could do crossword puzzles twice as fast if you could remember half of what you used to know.

You remember when they actually reported news on the nightly newscast.

• • • •

You take special notice of the days where nothing hurts.

You remember when it was actually possible to "Buy American."

• • • •

You know a store where they replace watch batteries.

Your favorite superhero, Middle-Aged Man, knows where the spare lightbulbs are, owns a full set of Torx drivers, and has a fully diversified portfolio, but he has yet to be invited to join the Justice League or the Avengers.

You're not sure what the difference is between the president and the CEO, even though you are both of them.

You've thought about how much landfill is dedicated just to burying your old socks and underwear.

You have a chair you sit in to eat, and no one else had better sit there.

• • • •

Turns out, even if you do study history, you're still doomed to repeat it.

• • • •

Your midlife crisis occurred when they stopped making the toothpaste you've used since 1971.

If they asked you, you'd say we won't be needing any more animated penguin movies for a while.

● ● ● ●

Even though your "baby" is now twenty-three, your wife still cuts her meat for her when she visits.

● ● ● ●

You're pretty sure if you had to start over, you wouldn't bother.

Considering how you feel about shuffleboard, bingo, and cruises, you figure your ancestors were lucky they didn't live past forty-five.

• • • •

You are the neighborhood authority on the impact of ill-timed national holidays on the trash collection schedule.

You once worked a cash register that did not calculate change or have buttons with pictures of every item for sale.

•   •   •   •

Your kids don't believe you when you tell them that in five years no one will care what they majored in.

You rode your bike to work, cut your grass with a manual mower, and lived without air-conditioning— before it was cool.

• • • • •

You know the Great Depression took place in the thirties, but you're a little less certain of the dates or names of any other depressions.

You've noticed that the spork has yet to make meaningful inroads into the American kitchen utensil drawer.

● ● ● ●

You've used the term "merit badge" and then had to explain it.

You know that "LOL," "ROTFL," and "IMHO" will inevitably join "ten-four," "23 skidoo," and "grotty" in the dustbin of history.

• • • •

When you went to high school, guys with pierced anything got beaten up, and a metal grill in your mouth was a guarantee that you'd remain a virgin until college.

Apparently those antiwar songs from the sixties didn't make as much of a sociopolitical impact as you once thought.

You remember when people got their news from the newspaper.

You wouldn't be
caught dead drinking
Colt 45, Champale,
or Boone's Farm.

• • • •

You remember
when all we had to save
were the whales.

You're no longer disappointed in the politicians, just the people who elect them.

You remember when there were no ratings on movies, warnings on cigarettes, or seat belts in cars.

When it comes to college courses, you're as liberal as the next guy, but the Study of Whiteness is beyond ridiculous.

• • • •

You remember when you could actually trust a news anchor.

Life may be a young man's game, but the referees are all middle-aged.

• • • •

You remember when branding was for cattle, spin was something you put on a backhand, and damage control was what the Merchant Marine did to avoid sinking.

When you apply for a passport, you bring every form of ID known to man.

• • • •

You're not getting older, you're getting bitter.

When your financial planner
suggested that you donate
your body to science,
you didn't realize he
meant immediately.

You're still interested
in the pursuit of happiness,
but you limit yourself
to one day a week.

You sneezed and threw out
your back for a week.

● ● ● ●

You're resigned to the
fact that any minor home-
repair job you undertake will
require at least three trips
to the Home Depot.

You never go to the DMV without an appointment.

• • • •

You can have an intelligent conversation about the difference between a Schedule A, Schedule C, and Schedule D.

• • • •

Teenagers call your clothes "old school."

Dead Before 40

Jim Croce • 30

James Dean • 24

Chris Farley • 33

Lou Gehrig • 37

Che Guevara • 39

Jean Harlow • 26

Joan of Arc • 19

Janis Joplin • 27

Andy Kaufman • 35

John Keats • 25

John F. Kennedy Jr. • 38

Sam Kinison • 38

Jayne Mansfield • 36

Bob Marley • 36

Keith Moon • 32

Jim Morrison • 27

Wolfgang Amadeus Mozart • 35

Nero • 30

Eva Perón • 33

River Phoenix • 23

Sylvia Plath • 30

Freddie Prinze Sr. • 22

Otis Redding • 26

Selena • 23

Tupac Shakur • 25

Anna Nicole Smith • 39

Stuart Sutcliffe • 21

Ritchie Valens • 17

Vincent van Gogh • 37

Instead of throwing all your receipts into a shoe box, you now carefully file them in envelopes once a week.

• • • •

You remember spending hours studying record-album cover art.

You have broken appliances
repaired rather than
buying new ones.

• • • •

You went into panic mode
because your car was towed
away, then you discovered
that you'd merely parked
it a block away.

You remember when movie theaters had ushers.

• • • •

You remember when they were called pizza parlors, ice cream parlors, and beauty parlors.

You know who said,
"The Eagle has landed."

• • • •

You remember the
Fuller Brush man.

A cheap digital camera has more memory than your first desktop computer did.

• • • •

As a teenager you read *Cat's Cradle, The Catcher in the Rye,* and *A Separate Peace* on your own.

You remember when the "usual gang of idiots" in *Mad* magazine included Don Martin, Mort Drucker, Al Jaffee, and Dave Berg.

• • • •

You know the rules to Monopoly, Scrabble, and Risk, and everybody knows you know them.

**When asked for advice,
you have a tendency
to chuckle.**

● ● ● ●

Your son's college cracked
your nest egg, and your
daughter's wedding cooked it.

● ● ● ●

**People are surprised to hear
that your parents are still alive.**

At rock concerts they don't bother to search your backpack.

• • • •

Pregnant women offer you their seat on the bus.

• • • •

No one wants to hear your assessment of the relative hotness of Britney, Paris, and Lindsay.

The last time you went
for a run, two neighbors
called an ambulance and
one called the police.

Your trifocals gave you
away when you were
checking out the FedEx guy.

You can still lift the weights in the gym. It's the damn bar they go on that's too heavy.

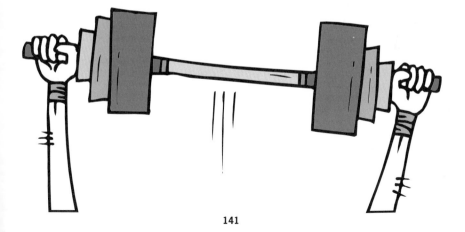

Four out of five dentists recommend you get crowns all around.

The nurse took your blood pressure three times, just to make sure the equipment hadn't malfunctioned.

You still haven't forgiven Milton Bradley for reversing the ranking scheme on Stratego.

• • • •

They decorated your birthday cake with the word *whatever*.

You can remember when
not having a television set
wasn't a lifestyle choice.

You think the Internet
and ATMs are cool, but
flush toilets are awesome.

You recall when the only readily available pornography was *National Geographic.*

• • • •

You remember when drinking water came from the tap.

Your body's plumbing makes more noise than the plumbing in your house.

•   •   •   •

You know the difference between stain, lacquer, shellac, and polyurethane.

You remember the advent
of the push-button phone.

You own a circular saw,
electric drill, and
electric sander.

You've chastised a teenager for text messaging in a movie theater.

• • • •

You're hanging on to your car, your job, and your spouse because you're too old to get new ones.

You remember when watermelons and grapes had seeds.

• • • •

You know how to operate the damper on a fireplace.

You own a dog-eared copy of *Hints from Heloise*.

• • • •

While driving your teenage daughter on a tour of various colleges, you seriously considered driving into oncoming traffic.

You place a stop order
on your mail and newspaper
delivery a week before
going on vacation.

You remember when
your hair was brown and
your teeth were white.

Your life insurance payment
could pay the mortgage
on a beach house.

• • • •

You're on your fifth passport.

• • • •

You've realized that
"multitasking" merely means
doing two things at the
same time—poorly.

You've never heard of any
of the bands at Lollapalooza.

•   •   •   •

Your closet was once organized
by mini, midi, and maxi.

•   •   •   •

Most of your favorite authors,
actors, and musicians are dead.

You still can't accept that
your Technics SP-10
direct-drive turntable
is now a museum piece.

. . . .

Given the proper dose
of margaritas, you can
still do the Hustle.

You can pack a carry-on
bag for a two-week trip.

• • • •

You don't care what
your credit score is,
but you can chart
your total cholesterol.

All things being equal, you'll take first-world toilets over old-world charm.

When promoters of a rock concert encourage the use of "protection," you assume they are referring to sunscreen.

Your living will authorizes euthanasia when you can no longer see well enough to pluck your eyebrows.

• • • •

You've wondered, "Whatever happened to Quaaludes?"

You know the origins
of the band names
Steely Dan, the Doors,
and Three Dog Night.

• • • •

You've come to the
conclusion that wisdom is
1 percent inspiration and
99 percent ability to
keep your mouth shut.

No matter how pervasive
they get, you will always
suck at video games.

• • • •

You'll use MapQuest, but
GPS navigation systems
threaten your virility.

Your pharmacist says flu shots are recommended for "people your age."

• • • •

If you had to live your life over, you'd demand your current rate of pay.

• • • •

You firmly believe the best things in life are free, and, of those, a good nap ranks near the top.

You're too old for Facebook,
too young for a face-lift.

• • • •

You can no longer read your
own handwriting.

• • • •

You've used the word
"pension" in
casual conversation.

You know what a
colostomy bag is.

You TiVo the
Weather Channel.

When they asked for volunteers to give up their seats on an overbooked flight in exchange for a free flight to anywhere in the forty-eight contiguous states, you turned down the offer because you were traveling with your spouse and two kids.

You have no idea who Franz Ferdinand, Guster, and Radiohead are.

• • • •

You remember when it was forbidden to use your Social Security number for identification purposes.

You've read *I'm Okay, You're Okay, Your Erroneous Zones,* and *Games People Play.*

• • • •

When they say the stock market made a correction, you know it really means the Dow Jones crashed.

You think a BlackBerry is a fruit.

• • • •

You remember who hosted *The Price Is Right* before Bob Barker.

You have no idea why anyone would want to text message when they could just as easily leave a voice mail.

• • • •

When asked what you expect to be doing in five years, you reply, "Screwing supermodels."

You've roller-skated to
the Captain and Tennille,
Electric Light Orchestra, and
Olivia Newton-John.

• • • •

If you're only as old
as you feel, "like hell"
must be about fifty-seven.

You tasted the sweet nectar
of the "empty nest"
only to have it cruelly
snatched away by the
"Boomerang Generation."

You remember what
Joan Rivers, Kenny Rogers,
and Michael Jackson
originally looked like.

You remember when people treated anxiety, depression, or impotency with alcohol.

• • • •

Now that they've banned smoking in movies, you can no longer determine when the characters just finished having sex.

Your first car had a carbon
footprint somewhere
between Mount Saint Helens
and Newark, New Jersey.

• • • •

You've actually done it
to the Meat Loaf song
"Two Out of Three Ain't Bad."

You're glad your kids
escaped the ignominy
of having their generation
named after a sugary cola.

•   •   •   •

"Hope I die before I get old":
one more thing you're not
going to accomplish.

You've come to the realization that whoever said there was more sex in the 1960s and 1970s should have been more specific.

• • • •

After decades of sitting too close to the TV, not eating carrots, and masturbating daily, it's a medical miracle you still have 20/20 vision.

Your eighty-year-old dad still wants to know when you plan on getting a "real job."

• • • •

You've reached the age where, legally, shorts can be worn only in the privacy of your own home.

• • • •

You've found solace in the fact that all men have that strange little patch on their shoulder where hair doesn't grow.

Now that you know what it's like
to be fifty, you're terrified that we
elected a president who was seventy.

• • • •

You remember when it was okay
to launch a trash can into low orbit
without risking a visit from the
Department of Homeland Security.

• • • •

You finally have a shot
at dating Ann-Margret,
Jane Fonda, or Ali MacGraw.

You're pretty sure there is a direct correlation between the invention of indoor plumbing and the ability to maintain the will to live past forty-five.

You know that John Mitchell, H. R. Haldeman, and John Ehrlichman were not members of Mötley Crüe.

• • • •

You know precisely when to shout out "No shit, Sherlock!" during a midnight showing of *The Rocky Horror Picture Show.*

You did the bump
to the hit disco song
"Push Push in the Bush."

●   ●   ●   ●

You remember
when Bobby Fischer
and Anatoly Karpov were
treated like superstars.

You're appalled that your teenage daughter thinks Khmer Rouge is made by L'Oréal and the fall of Saigon is a fashion show.

You still wonder where Jimmy Hoffa went.

You remember when Bruce Springsteen appeared on the cover of *Time* and *Newsweek* in the same week and was billed as the new Bob Dylan.

• • • •

You know who Squeaky Fromme, Patty Hearst, and Clifford Irving are.

You've said "and Francisco Franco is still dead" in a meeting and received blank stares from the twentysomethings in the room.

• • • •

In your high school graduation picture, you have a mullet or a Jheri Curl.

You're still waiting for a
Duran Duran reunion.

• • • •

You wonder why
Boy George still goes
by that name.

Now that you're permitted to
address your parents' friends
by their first names, you avoid
calling them anything at all.

• • • •

You fondly remember when
Dan Quayle attacked
the fictional character
Murphy Brown for lacking
family values.

You remember when airplane and bus passengers were allowed to smoke in the back rows.

When a teenager says "TMI," you think of Three Mile Island.

You owned the first Macintosh computer, which you've stored in the original box in your garage as a collector's item.

At one time you actually thought Commodore and Atari would rule the world.

You can still hum the theme songs from Donkey Kong, Ms. Pac Man, and Space Invaders.

You went to work dressed like a character from the movie *Flashdance* or the television show *Miami Vice*.

• • • •

You remember the faces of the original VJs on MTV, but you can't remember any of their names—except for Martha Quinn.

You still own a copy
of Michael Jackson's
Thriller LP.

• • • •

You know the proper
response to the question
"Who you gonna call?"

You know who John
Anderson, Ross Perot,
and Abe Beam are.

• • • •

You remember
Day 220 of America
Held Hostage.

You know the difference between Garry Trudeau and Pierre Trudeau.

You love the fact that Evian spelled backward is Naive.

What Others Say About Middle Age

"In a man's middle years there is scarcely
a part of the body he would hesitate
to turn over to the proper authorities."
—E. B. White

"Old age is fifteen years older than I am."
—Oliver Wendell Holmes

•

"There is still no cure for the common birthday."
—John Glenn

•

"The first half of our lives is ruined by our parents, and the second half by our children."
—Clarence Darrow

•

"Middle age is when you've met so many people that every new person you meet reminds you of someone else."
—Ogden Nash

"At twenty we worry about what others think of us; at forty we don't care about what others think of us; at sixty we discover they haven't been thinking about us at all."
—Malcolm Forbes

•

"Middle age is when you still believe you'll feel better in the morning."
—Bob Hope

•

"The secret of staying young is to live honestly, eat slowly, and lie about your age."
—Lucille Ball

"Age is not a particularly interesting subject.
Anyone can get old.
All you have to do is live long enough."
—Groucho Marx

•

"Age is a very high price to pay for maturity."
—Tom Stoppard

•

"True terror is to wake up one morning
and discover that your high school class
is running the country."
—Kurt Vonnegut

•

"The really frightening thing about middle age
is the knowledge that you'll grow out of it."
—Doris Day

In the wake of America's 2001 invasion of Afghanistan, you found it ironic that the United States boycotted the 1980 Summer Olympics in Moscow to protest the Russian invasion of Afghanistan.

• • • •

You remember when there were countries named Rhodesia, Zaire, and Cambodia.

You knew who Salman Rushdie was before Iran called for his death.

• • • •

When Pope John Paul I died after only thirty-three days as pope, you dressed up as a nun for Halloween.

When you told the salesperson at the Apple Store that you owned the first Macintosh computer, she replied, "That was way before I was born."

• • • •

You know Son of Sam's real name.

• • • •

You remember how and when Richard Pryor set himself on fire.

You can pronounce
Lech Walesa.

•   •   •   •

You remember when
Daniel Ortega was president
of Nicaragua the first time.

•   •   •   •

You once longed to own
a DeLorean.

**No matter the brand,
style, or color, you just
do not look cool in shorts.**

● ● ● ●

**You know the name
of "the guy who died"
in every rock band
from 1958 to 1975.**

You remember when Watergate was just a hotel, Vietnam was just a country, and Kool-Aid was just an artificially flavored powdered drink.

Your experience with the draft lottery had nothing to do with the NBA or basketball.

It's legal for you
to date women
half your age.

• • • •

What's worse
than gray hair?
Gray pubic hair.

You remember when cheap imports came from Japan.

You're on your fourth dog and your third cat.

You believe that whoever linked the words "reality" and "TV" did not firmly grasp either concept.

● ● ● ●

Your muscles
have wrinkles.

You stopped showing off your "full-body scan" after the people in the office asked if radiation shrinks one's private parts.

You consider a game of chess an exciting activity.

• • • •

You know that the Everly Brothers were brothers, the Righteous Brothers weren't, the Allman Brothers were, the Doobie Brothers weren't, and the Isley Brothers were.

You nearly had a heart attack
when you heard someone say,
"I grew up listening to
Kelly Clarkson."

● ● ● ●

**You have meaningful
conversations with your mailman.**

● ● ● ●

You've stopped looking at your ass
in the mirror because you're
resigned to the fact that it isn't
going to get any better.

You gave up your electric toothbrush because you needed the exercise.

• • • •

Your "contact" list is recorded in pencil in a compact leather directory.

• • • •

If they made "quadfocals," you'd probably need them.

There's no junk in your trunk but the spare tire, the jack, and jumper cables.

• • • •

Just once you'd like to buy running shoes that don't look like they came from Flash Gordon's closet.

You remember the years when *Saturday Night Live* was funny, unfunny, funny again, unfunny again, funny . . .

• • • •

No, you can't use the baby changing room to change your own diaper.

Your Rolodex has been collecting dust in a closet for the last fifteen years.

• • • •

You're convinced *High School Musical* is just another Frankie Avalon movie.

You've seriously considered taking an American Express bus tour of the Czech Republic, which you still refer to as Czechoslovakia.

• • • •

You've finally resigned yourself to carrying your toolbox upstairs when having to make a repair job, instead of making six trips back and forth to the garage.

You no longer
consider the words
"hernia" or "hemorrhoid"
amusing whatsoever.

• • • •

You long for the days
when there was only one
version of Monopoly.

You've come to the
conclusion that if you had
to apply to college today,
you'd be rejected by
your alma mater.

You've seriously considered
having GPS surgically
implanted into your teenager.

You've calculated the investment potential of hoarding first-class "forever stamps."

•   •   •   •

You're perplexed to learn that colleges now offer a major in Peace Studies.

You think phone sex requires using the receiver to conduct a pelvic exam.

You still cringe when you recall that Bill Clinton used a song by Fleetwood Mac as his campaign song.

Dick Cheney reminds you of your high school vice principal. Karl Rove reminds you of your junior high school shop teacher.

You once wore a leisure suit and thought you were "stylin'."

You yearn for a Winnebago.

• • • •

You knew John Kerry wasn't going to win the presidency the moment you heard his wife's foreign accent.

You're convinced there's nothing quite like a good game of Chinese checkers.

• • • •

You tip well.

• • • •

You get vertigo when you get halfway up a rock-climbing wall.

You know it's inevitable that commercial-free satellite radio will eventually be cluttered with commercials.

• • • •

You've got floaters.

• • • •

You enjoy tours of historical landmarks and presidential museums.

You've mastered the art of doing your laundry without turning your underwear gray.

• • • •

When you watch reruns of *All in the Family*, you reluctantly find yourself agreeing with Archie.

You remember when the biggest threat to civilization was aerosol spray cans.

• • • •

You wonder why they banned Internet gambling but online stock trades are perfectly legal.

One more jury duty
summons and you get
a free DUI.

•   •   •   •

You wonder how long before
Microsoft, Google, and
Yahoo! will be overtaken by
foreign competition.

If you'd invested $1,000 with Warren Buffet in the 1950s, it would be worth over $26 million today.
Too bad you didn't.

• • • •

In choosing a dog, temperament and intelligence take a backseat to potential poop production.

The program for your college reunion lists two pages of dead people.

• • • •

You remember when the only person "making six figures" was the Man.

Everything you needed to know, you learned from Captain Kangaroo.

• • • •

As a kid, you drank water from a garden hose.

• • • •

"Dude, I swear to God, Sha Na Na performed at Woodstock. You can look it up."

You've heard words come
out of your mouth that sound
exactly like your father.

• • • • •

You remember when
Nelson Rockefeller gave
the press the finger.

• • • • •

You leave Post-it notes around the
house so you'll remember to pick
up one of your kids from a playdate.

You have boxes of old business cards from jobs you left decades ago.

You replace the air-conditioning filters on a regular basis.

You know the difference between a treasury bill, a treasury note, and a municipal bond.

● ● ● ●

You've had a wart surgically removed.

You always wear flip-flops
in hotel showers.

• • • •

You bought a plumber's
snake, but you have no idea
how to properly use it.

You've called the police
to quiet down
a neighbor's party.

• • • •

You get more phone calls
from telemarketers
than friends.

You have life insurance.

• • • •

You've located old friends
through the Internet,
reestablished contact,
and then remembered
why you lost contact
in the first place.

You no longer look good
in a tank top.

●　●　●　●

You own a corkscrew that
was designed by NASA.

You still look things up
in the encyclopedia.

● ● ● ●

You know who Kilgore Trout is.

● ● ● ●

You know it's just a matter
of time before all your DVDs
are obsolete.

You've turned into
your parents.

• • • •

You're still uncomfortable
with German reunification.

• • • •

You've said, "That's a Rube
Goldberg contraption,"
and received blank stares.

A poster of David or Shaun Cassidy once hung in your bedroom.

You refuse to buy an iPhone until you figure out how to work your iPod.

Most of the utensils in your kitchen drawers have been used only once.

• • • •

You've had the urge to smash a Furby with a sledgehammer.

You remember when the
IBM Selectric II was the
most awesome typewriter
on the planet.

• • • •

You refuse to buy the book
*1,000 Places to See Before
You Die* because you realized
you just don't have time
to travel to more than
thirty-seven of them.

You know how to use
a typewriter.

• • • •

At home, you put on
a cardigan sweater
and slippers, just like
Mr. Rogers.

You've considered buying a grave site, but you decided instead to embrace denial.

You've been pulled over by the police for going too slow.

You think any song
by 50 Cent isn't worth
even that much.

You're consoled by action
movies in which Harrison Ford,
Sean Connery, or Tommy Lee
Jones has a love interest
who is in her thirties.

You wouldn't be caught dead sitting in a car with the windows rolled down and hip-hop blasting.

●　●　●　●

You no longer think that driving a red Ferrari will help you pick up chicks.

You have a living will,
but you refuse to give
your teenager control
over who pulls the plug
on your iron lung.

• • • •

You go to church
without a fight.

You've apologized to your
parents for your behavior
as a teenager.

•   •   •   •

You no longer have
to go looking for trouble.
It finds you.

•   •   •   •

You've refused to accept
someone's business card.

You've attended Lamaze class, back-to-school night, and a time-share seminar.

• • • •

You threw your back out during sex, but you told the doctor you were changing the oil filter on your car.

• • • •

They played "Wild Thing," "Mellow Yellow," and "Doo Wah Diddy Diddy" at your prom.

You complained
when a gallon of gas
cost forty-nine cents.

• • • •

Your preferred biofuel
is Flower Power.

You lived through the
Silent Spring, the Summer
of Love, and the
Winter of Discontent.

You learned to drive without
power brakes, power
steering, or power seats.

You got to second base watching *Smokey and the Bandit* at the drive-in.

Between the Pill, the Sexual Revolution, and Viagra, you figure we are "The Best-Laid Generation."

You've realized that there aren't enough years left in your life to let compound interest turn you into a billionaire.